Bugs in My Backyard

I See
Dragonflies

By Julia Jaske

I see a dragonfly.

I see a pink dragonfly.

4

I see a blue dragonfly.

I see a dragonfly flying.

I see a dragonfly exploring.

I see a dragonfly waiting.

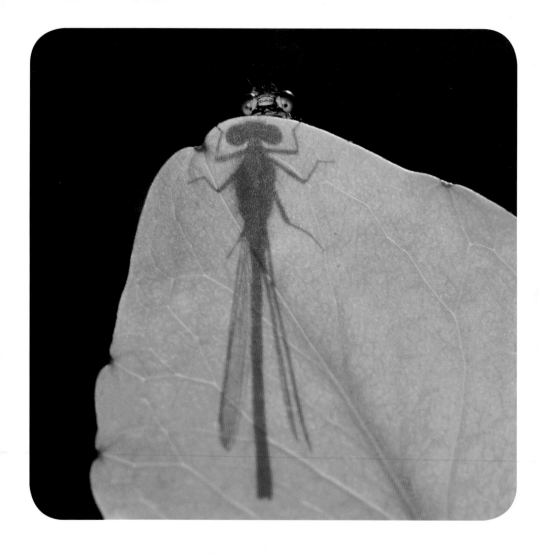

I see a dragonfly hiding.

I see a dragonfly smelling.

I see a dragonfly playing.

I see a dragonfly resting.

12 I see a dragonfly splashing.

I see a dragonfly saying hello!

Word List

dragonfly
pink
blue
flying
exploring
waiting
hiding

smelling
playing
resting
splashing
saying
hello

I see a dragonfly.

I see a pink dragonfly.

I see a blue dragonfly.

I see a dragonfly flying.

I see a dragonfly exploring.

I see a dragonfly waiting.

I see a dragonfly hiding.

I see a dragonfly smelling.

I see a dragonfly playing.

I see a dragonfly resting.

I see a dragonfly splashing.

I see a dragonfly saying hello!

CHERRY BLOSSOM PRESS

Published in the United States of America by Cherry Lake Publishing Group
Ann Arbor, Michigan
www.cherrylakepublishing.com

Book Designer: Melinda Millward

Photo Credits: ©Rudmer Zwerver/Shutterstock.com, front cover, 1; ©Hintau Aliaksei/Shutterstock.com, back cover, 14; ©kesipun/Shutterstock.com, 2; ©Nayk Karlson/Shutterstock.com, 3; ©Michael Reilly/Shutterstock.com, 4; ©Philip Hunton/Shutterstock.com, 5; ©Svetlana Orusova/Shutterstock.com, 6; ©Parsha/Shutterstock.com, 7; ©Savo Ilic/Shutterstock.com, 8; ©niwatn.th/Shutterstock.com, 9; ©lessysebastian/Shutterstock.com, 10; ©Aleks Kvintet/Shutterstock.com, 11; ©VyacheslavLn/Shutterstock.com, 12; ©Roman Stavytskyi/Shutterstock.com, 13

Cherry Blossom Press is an imprint of Cherry Lake Publishing Group.

Library of Congress Cataloging-in-Publication Data

Names: Jaske, Julia, author.
Title: I see dragonflies / by Julia Jaske.
Description: Ann Arbor, Michigan : Cherry Lake Publishing, 2022. | Series: Bugs in my backyard | Audience: Grades K-1
Identifiers: LCCN 2021036405 (print) | LCCN 2021036406 (ebook) | ISBN 9781534198852 (paperback) | ISBN 9781668905753 (ebook) | ISBN 9781668901434 (pdf)
Subjects: LCSH: Dragonflies—Juvenile literature.
Classification: LCC QL520 .J37 2022 (print) | LCC QL520 (ebook) | DDC 595.7/33—dc23
LC record available at https://lccn.loc.gov/2021036405
LC ebook record available at https://lccn.loc.gov/2021036406

Cherry Lake Publishing Group would like to acknowledge the work of the Partnership for 21st Century Learning, a Network of Battelle for Kids. Please visit http://www.battelleforkids.org/networks/p21 for more information.

Printed in the United States of America
Corporate Graphics